Piano • Vocal • Guitar

DISCARDED

OUR GOD REIGNS

The Praise and Worship Collection

ISBN 0-7935-3833-5

HAL•LEONARD®
CORPORATION
7777 W. BLUEMOUND RD. P.O. BOX 13819 MILWAUKEE, WI 53213

Visit Hal Leonard Online at
www.halleonard.com

Piano • Vocal • Guitar

OUR GOD REIGNS

The Praise and Worship Collection

AMEN! PRAISE AND GLORY

Words and Music by
CHARLIE PEACOCK

AWESOME GOD

Words and Music by
RICH MULLINS

13

BETHLEHEM MORNING

Words and Music by
MORRIS CHAPMAN

BLESS HIS HOLY NAME

Words and Music by
ANDRAÉ CROUCH

EL SHADDAI

Words and Music by MICHAEL CARD
and JOHN THOMPSON

Through the years — you made — it clear — that the time —

— of Christ —was near, — though the peo - ple could - n't see —

EXALT THE NAME

Words and Music by MARGARET BECKER
and MARK HAUTH

FIND US FAITHFUL

Words and Music by
JON MOHR

pil-grims on ___ the jour-ney of the nar-row road, ___ and

42

FOR THE SAKE OF THE CALL

Words and Music by
STEVEN CURTIS CHAPMAN

GIVE THANKS

Words and Music by
HENRY SMITH

Gently

Give thanks with a grate-ful heart._ Give thanks to the Ho-ly One._ Give thanks _____ be-cause He's giv-en Je-sus Christ, _____ His Son. Give

GREAT IS THE LORD

Words and Music by MICHAEL W. SMITH
and DEBORAH D. SMITH

56

GOD WILL MAKE A WAY

Words and Music by
DON MOEN

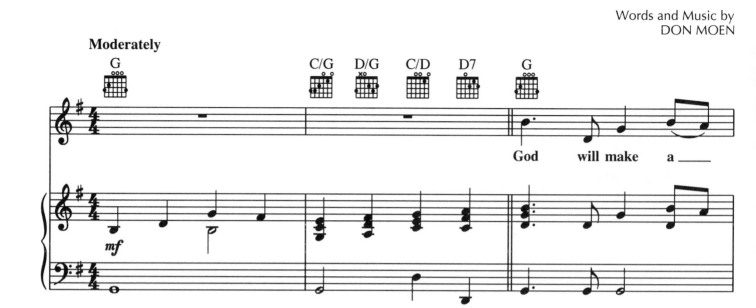

God will make a ___

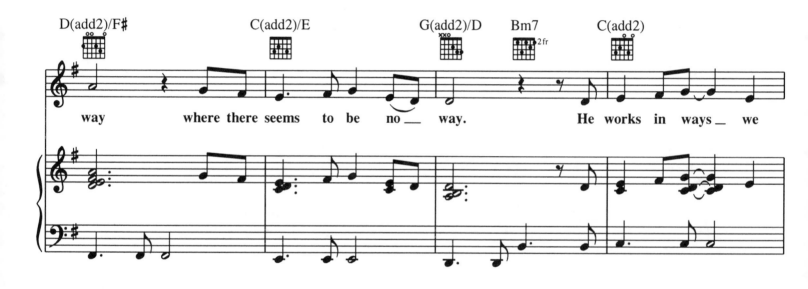

way where there seems to be no ___ way. He works in ways ___ we

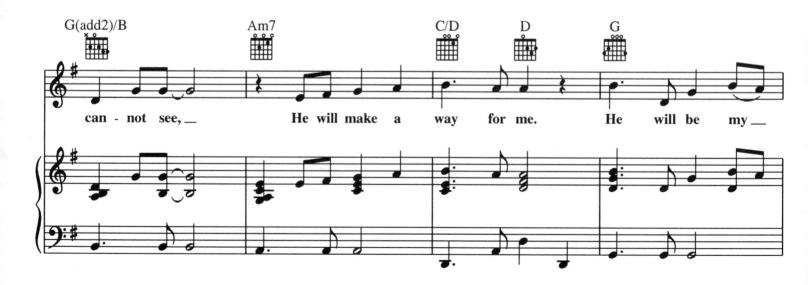

can - not see, ___ He will make a way for me. He will be my ___

60

64

HE WHO BEGAN A GOOD WORK IN YOU

Words and Music by
JON MOHR

HE WILL CARRY YOU

Words and Music by
SCOTT WESLEY BROWN

Moderately

There is no prob - lem too big He can - not

solve it; _____ there is no moun - tain too

HIS EYES

Words and Music by STEVEN CURTIS CHAPMAN
and JAMES ISAAC ELLIOTT

CODA

day, to - day! 3. Some - times I look a - bove me when stars are shin - ing,____ and I feel so small. How could the God__ of heav - en and all cre - a - tion____ know I'm here at all?____ But then in the si - lence He whis - pers,__ "My child, I cre - a - ted you

HIS STRENGTH IS PERFECT

Words and Music by STEVEN CURTIS CHAPMAN
and JERRY SALLEY

HOLY GROUND

Words and Music by
GERON DAVIS

86

HOLY GROUND

Words and Music by
CHRISTOPHER BEATTY

HOW MAJESTIC IS YOUR NAME

Words and Music by
MICHAEL W. SMITH

O Lord,___ our Lord,___ how ma-

94

95

I EXALT THEE

Words and Music by
PETE SANCHEZ, JR.

I HAVE DECIDED

Words and Music by
MICHAEL CARD

I WANT TO FOLLOW YOU

Words and Music by
CHERI KEAGGY

I LOVE YOU LORD

Words and Music by
LAURIE KLEIN

IMMANUEL

Words and Music by
MICHAEL CARD

114

IN SPIRIT AND IN TRUTH

Words and Music by
CHARLIE PEACOCK

IN CHRIST ALONE

Words and Music by DON KOCH
and SHAWN CRAIG

In Christ a - lone _

_ will I glo - ry, though I could pride my - self in bat - tles
_ will I glo - ry, for on - ly by His grace I am re -

won. For I've been blessed be - yond meas - ure, and by His strength a - lone I o - ver -
deemed. And on - ly His ten - der mer - cy could reach be - yond my weak - ness to my

124

cross. _____ In ev - 'ry vic - to - ry let it be said of _ me: My

source of strength, _____ my source of hope _____ is Christ a - lone. My

source of strength, _____ my source of hope is Christ a - lone, _____

is Christ a - lone! _____

JEHOVAH
(a/k/a NEVER LET YOU GO)

Words and Music by
GEOFFREY P. THURMAN

Flowing, with purpose ♩ = 138

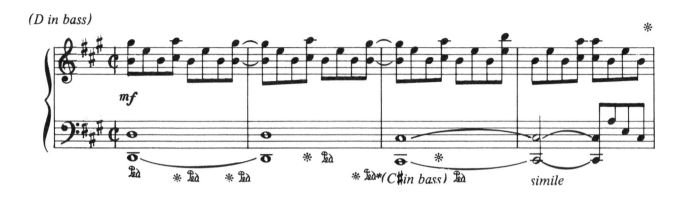

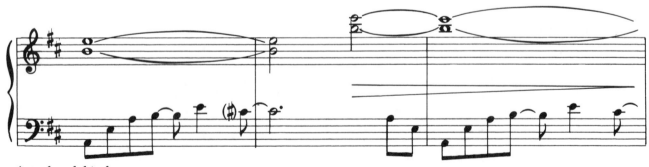

* end pedal in bass

1. Con - sid - er the lil - ies of the field, ____
(2.) sid - er the crea - tures of the air, ____
(3.) sid - er the lil - ies of the field, ____

cued notes: 2nd time

____ for Sol - o - mon dressed in roy - al robe ____
____ for all of the dia - monds in all ____
____ for how much more does He love His own, ____

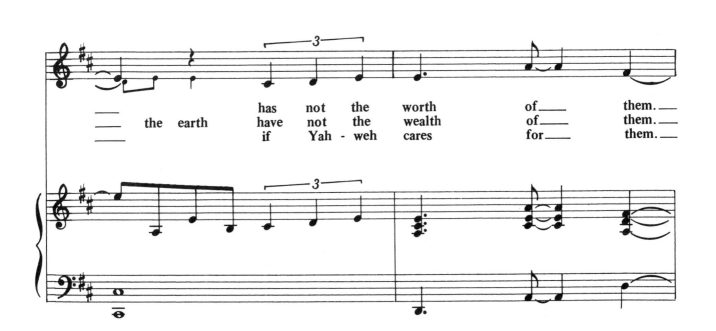

____ the earth has not the worth of ____ them. ____
____ the earth have not the wealth of ____ them. ____
____ if Yah - weh cares for ____ them. ____

128

134

*(C♯ in bass)

Repeat and fade   Optional ending

Nev - er   let   you ——

(C♮ in bass)

mp

(B in bass)

tenuto   L.H.

ritard

JESUS IS THE ANSWER

Words and Music by ANDRAÉ CROUCH
and SANDRA CROUCH

JESUS, LORD TO ME

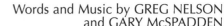

Words and Music by GREG NELSON
and GARY McSPADDEN

141

144

145

LIFT UP A SONG

Words and Music by
STEVE FRY

150

MAJESTY

Words and Music by
JACK W. HAYFORD

MY TRIBUTE
(a/k/a TO GOD BE THE GLORY)

Words and Music by
ANDRAÉ CROUCH

O HOW HE LOVES YOU AND ME

Words and Music by
KURT KAISER

Gospel Waltz tempo

Oh, how He loves you and me! _____

Oh, how He loves you and me! _____

He gave His life, what _ more could He give?

OH LORD, YOU'RE BEAUTIFUL

Words and Music by
KEITH GREEN

166

O MAGNIFY THE LORD

Words and Music by MELODIE TUNNEY
and DICK TUNNEY

mag-ni-fy, ___ O mag-ni-fy ___ the Lord ___ with me, ___ and
(2) wor-ship Him, ___ O wor-ship Christ, the Lord ___ with me, ___ and

174

OUR GOD REIGNS

Words and Music by
LEONARD SMITH

178

PROCLAIM THE GLORY OF THE LORD

Words and Music by DWIGHT LILES
and NILES BOROP

184

PRAISE THE NAME OF JESUS

Words and Music by
ROY HICKS, JR.

187

REVIVE US, O LORD

Words and Music by
STEVE CAMP and CARMAN

193

SAY THE NAME

Words and Music by MARGARET BECKER
and CHARLIE PEACOCK

Flowing in four

A more sweet - er sound - ing____ word these____
nev - er grow so____ strong that my

lips have nev - er____ said; A gen - tle name____ so beau-
heart can - not be____ moved; May I nev - er____ grow____

SIMPLE SONG FOR A MIGHTY GOD

Words and Music by CLAIRE CLONINGER
and KEITH THOMAS

1. He spread the stars a-cross the night, and built His pal-ace in the heav-ens.
2. Wrapped in robes of light, He brought cre-a-tion in-to be-ing,

SPIRIT OF THE LIVING GOD

Words and Music by DANIEL IVERSON
and LOWELL ALEXANDER

SING YOUR PRAISE TO THE LORD

Words and Music by
RICHARD MULLINS

Adapted from J.S.Bach's Fugue No.2 in C minor,WTC Vol.I

In a steady four, with excitement ♩=88

sing, sing, ___ sing, let me hear ya now, sing, sing, ___ sing. _____

THANK YOU

Words and Music by
RAY BOLTZ

THERE IS JOY IN THE LORD

Words and Music by CHERI KEAGGY

THY WORD

Words and Music by AMY GRANT
and MICHAEL W. SMITH

Based on Psalm 119:105

With meaning ♩ = 80

*Guitar chords
are up a half step*

Thy Word is a lamp un-to my feet and a light un-to my path.

cued note 4th time

(Now)

Coda

Noth- ing will I fear as long as you are near.

Please be near me to the end.

Thy Word is a lamp un-to my feet and a

1.

light un - to my path.

VIA DOLOROSA

Words and Music by BILLY SPRAGUE
and NILES BOROP

WE TRUST IN THE NAME OF THE LORD OUR GOD

Words and Music by
STEVEN CURTIS CHAPMAN

Some trust_ in char - i - ots; we
Some trust_ in the work they do; we

trust in the name of the Lord our_ God. Some trust_ in hors - es; we
trust in the name of the Lord our_ God. 'Cause by His grace_ all the work is through; we

trust in the name of the Lord our_ God.
trust in the name of the Lord our_ God.

We trust_ in the name of the Lord our

WE WILL GLORIFY

Words and Music by
TWILA PARIS

1. We will glo - ri - fy the
(2) ho - vah reigns in

240

WE WILL STAND
(YOU'RE MY BROTHER, YOU'RE MY SISTER)

Words and Music by RUSS TAFF, TORI TAFF
and JAMES HOLLIHAN

Slowly, but with a beat ♩ =66

Some - times __ it's hard __ for me to un - der - stand _____ why we

WORTHY IS THE LAMB

Words and Music by
MORRIS CHAPMAN

The Finest In Inspirational Music

America's Gospel Top Forty
40 of the most popular gospel songs ever to hit the Gospel Top Forty, including: God Bless The U.S.A. • I Bowed On My Knees And Cried Holy • More Than Wonderful • Somebody Touched Me • many more. Arranged for piano/guitar/4-part vocal.
00359061 ....$8.95

Climb Ev'ry Mountain
Over 130 songs: Day By Day • One Day At A Time • Bridge Over Troubled Water • Let There Be Peace On Earth • Gonna Build A Mountain • The Old Rugged Cross • Rock Of Ages • Abide With Me • Nearer, My God, To Thee • What A Friend We Have In Jesus.
00312100 ....$16.95

Country Gospel U.S.A.
50 songs written for piano/guitar/four-part vocal. Highlights: Daddy Sang Bass • He Set Me Free • I Saw The Light • Kum Ba Yah • Mansion Over The Hilltop • Love Lifted Me • Turn Your Radio On • When The Saints Go Marching In • many others.
00240139 ....$9.95

Favorite Hymns
71 all-time favorites, including: Abide With Me • Amazing Grace • Ave Maria • Christ The Lord Is Risen Today • Faith Of Our Fathers • In The Sweet By And By • Jesus Loves Me! • Just A Closer Walk With Thee • A Mighty Fortress Is Our God • Onward Christian Soldiers • Rock Of Ages • Swing Low, Sweet Chariot • Were You There? • and many more!
00490436 ....$12.95

Glorious Praise
Great Songwriters & Songs
24 songs, including: Find A Way • Friends • How Majestic Is Your Name • O Magnify The Lord • Via Dolorosa • The Warrior Is A Child.
00359895 ....$10.95

Great Gospel Songs Of Thomas A. Dorsey
37 of his greatest songs, including: There'll Be Peace In The Valley (For Me) • Take My Hand Precious Lord • Say A Little Prayer For Me • Someway, Somehow, Sometime, Somewhere • There Is No Friend Like Jesus.
00359946 ....$7.95

Gregorian Chant
This centuries-old art form is regaining popularity as people discover its free-flowing rhythms and haunting melodies. This one-of-a-kind collection includes 23 beautiful and celestial plainchants for a capella voice.
00310003 ....$8.95

The New Illustrated Family Hymn Book
Featuring designs from the Hallmark Collection
A collector's edition for everyone who loves hymns. This deluxe album features a history of the hymn from its Old Testament origins and 50 of the world's most popular hymns for piano, organ or electronic keyboard. Each hymn is presented with an account of its history and a magnificent four-color design selected from the archives of Hallmark Cards. The greatest Christian hymns are included, such as: Abide With Me • Amazing Grace • How Great Thou Art • In The Garden • The Old Rugged Cross • What A Friend We Have In Jesus. Includes 50 full-color photos!
00183297 ....$19.95

Favorites Of Mahalia Jackson
15 favorites of the world's greatest gospel singer: Amazing Grace • God Spoke To Me One Day • I Can Put My Trust In Jesus • Move On Up A Little Higher • What Could I Do If It Wasn't For The Lord? • more. Includes biography.
00307150 ....$5.95

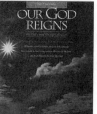

The New Young Messiah
Matching folio to the album featuring top Contemporary Christian artists performing a modern rendition of Handel's *Messiah*. Features Sandy Patty, Steven Curtis Chapman, Larnelle Harris, and others.
00310006 ....$16.95

Our God Reigns
50 classics, including: Awesome God • El Shaddai • He Will Carry You • How Majestic Is Your Name • Jesus Is The Answer • O Magnify The Lord • Say The Name • Thank You • Via Dolorosa • and more.
00311695 ....$17.95

Praise
25 selections: Behold The Lamb • El Shaddai • How Majestic Is Your Name • Praise The Lord • Sweet, Sweet Spirit • Through His Eyes • Worthy The Lamb • many more.
00240775 ....$8.95

Songs Of Worship And Praise
18 songs, including: El Shaddai • How Majestic Is Your Name • The King Of Who I Am • There's Something About That Name • Worthy The Lamb.
00361131 ....$7.95

Gospel
The Ultimate Series
A collection of 100 of the most inspirational gospel songs ever, featuring: Because He Lives • Climb Ev'ry Mountain • Daddy Sang Bass • Everything Is Beautiful • For Loving Me • He • He Touched Me • He's Got The Whole World In His Hands • His Eye Is On The Sparrow • Home Where I Belong • How Great Thou Art • I Saw The Light • Just A Closer Walk With Thee • Just Any Day Now • Kum Ba Yah • Mansion Over The Hilltop • Old Rugged Cross • Peace In The Valley • Put Something Back • Rock Of Ages • Sincerely Yours • The Singer • The Sun's Coming Up • Take My Hand, Precious Lord • Without Him • more.
00241009 ....$17.95

FOR MORE INFORMATION, SEE YOUR LOCAL MUSIC DEALER, OR WRITE TO:

HAL•LEONARD™ CORPORATION
7777 W. BLUEMOUND RD. P.O. BOX 13819 MILWAUKEE, WI 53213

Prices, contents, and availability subject to change without notice.
Some products may not be available outside the U.S.A.

The Greatest Collections Of Sacred Music

These books feature melody line, lyrics, and chords for hundreds of your favorite inspirational songs.

The Very Best Of Contemporary Christian Words & Music

More than 400 contemporary Christian songs including: Angels • Bread On The Water • Coloring Song • Doubly Good • El Shaddai • Everywhere I Go • Father's Eyes • Find A Way • He's Alive • Heart Of The Seeker • Home Where I Belong • How Majestic Is Your Name • I Am Sure • I Have Decided • I'd Rather Believe In You • Lamb Of Glory • Love Calling • Love Found A Way • Rubble • Pour On The Power • Praise The Lord • The Sky's The Limit • Straight Ahead • Via Dolorosa • Vital Signs • The Warrior Is A Child • Was It A Morning Like This • Wise Up • and hundreds more. Handy plastic-comb binding. Includes 3 multi-indexing systems and guitar chord frames.
00240067 ....$24.95

Gospel's Best – Words & Music

The best reference book of gospel music ever compiled! Here are more than 500 songs, representing all areas of gospel music: traditional, spiritual, inspirational and contemporary. Guitar chord frames are included for each song. For ease of title location, two convenient listings of the songs are provided. Alphabetical Listing: Song titles are listed alphabetically. Music Composer & Lyricist Index: All music composer and lyricist names are listed individually in alphabetical sequence, followed by their respective songs. Songs include: Amazing Grace • Church In The Wildwood • Daddy Sang Bass • Everything Is Beautiful • He • He Touched Me • He's Got The Whole World In His Hands • His Name Is Wonderful • I Saw The Light • In The Garden • Just A Closer Walk With Thee • Praise The Lord • The Secret Place • Sing Your Praise To The Lord • Stubborn Love • Take My Hand, Precious Lord • A Thing Called Love • Through It All • Turn Your Radio On • We Shall Behold Him • Who Am I • Why Me, Lord? • more. For piano, organ, guitar and all "C" instruments. Handy plastic-comb binding.
00240048 ....$24.95

FOR MORE INFORMATION, SEE YOUR LOCAL MUSIC DEALER,
OR WRITE TO:

HAL•LEONARD™
CORPORATION
7777 W. BLUEMOUND RD. P.O. BOX 13819 MILWAUKEE, WI 53213

Prices, contents, and availability subject to change without notice.
Some products may not be available outside the U.S.A.

The Most Romantic Music In The World

The Best Love Songs Ever
Over 60 all-time favorites, updated to include recent hits. Features: Always • Anniversary Song • Beautiful In My Eyes • Can't Help Falling In Love • Can't Smile Without You • Could I Have This Dance • Don't Know Much • Endless Love • Have I Told You Lately • How Deep Is Your Love • I.O.U. • Just The Way You Are • Longer • Love Me Tender • Misty • She Believes In Me • Sunrise, Sunset • Till • Try To Remember • Vision Of Love • When I Fall In Love • You Needed Me • Your Song.
00359198 ....$17.95

The Big Book Of Love And Wedding Songs
81 romantic classics, contemporary favorites, and sacred standards in one convenient collection, including: All I Ask Of You • Anniversary Song • Ave Maria • Could I Have This Dance • Endless Love • Forever And Ever, Amen • Longer • Lost In Your Eyes • Sunrise, Sunset • You Decorated My Life • and more.
00311567 ....$19.95

The Definitive Love Collection
Over 100 sentimental favorites in one collection! Includes: All I Ask Of You • Can't Help Falling In Love • (They Long To Be) Close To You • Endless Love • The Glory Of Love • Have I Told You Lately That I Love You • Here And Now • I've Got My Love To Keep Me Warm • Isn't It Romantic? • It Could Happen To You • Let's Fall In Love • Love Me Tender • Save The Best For Last • So In Love • Somewhere Out There • A Time For Us • Unforgettable • When I Fall In Love • A Whole New World (Aladdin's Theme) • and more.
00311681 ....$27.95

Contemporary Love & Wedding Songs
26 songs of romance, including: Can't Help Falling In Love • Could I Have This Dance • Endless Love • I.O.U. • Just The Way You Are • Longer • Somewhere Out There • Sunrise, Sunset • Through The Years • You Needed Me • Your Song.
00359498........................$12.95

The New Complete Wedding Songbook
41 of the most requested and beloved songs for romance and weddings. Features: And This Is My Beloved • Anniversary Song • The Anniversary Waltz • Ave Maria • Can't Help Falling In Love • Canon in D (Pachelbel) • Could I Have This Dance • Endless Love • Feelings • For All We Know • The Hawaiian Wedding Song • How Deep Is Your Love • I Just Fall In Love Again • I Love You Truly • If We Only Have Love • Just The Way You Are • Let Me Call You Sweetheart • Longer • The Lord's Prayer • Love Me Tender • Love's Grown Deep • Melody of Love • Sunrise, Sunset • Through The Years • Too Much Heaven • True Love • Try To Remember • When I Need You • Whither Thou Goest • You Needed Me • You're My Everything • Your Song • and more.
00309326 ....$12.95

Isn't It Romantic?
A Treasury Of Classic Love Songs
50 romantic favorites, including: All The Things You Are • Body And Soul • If Ever I Would Leave You • Isn't It Romantic? • Misty • My Romance • The Nearness Of You • Smoke Gets In Your Eyes • The Very Thought Of You • and more.
00310009 ....$14.95

New Ultimate Love & Wedding Songbook
We've updated the "ultimate" to include even more of the greatest love songs ever written. More than 85 songs, including: And I Love Her • Could I Have This Dance? • Endless Love • Here, There And Everywhere • Just The Way You Are • Longer • Misty • One Hand, One Heart • Somewhere • Sunrise, Sunset • Through The Years • You Needed Me • more.
00361445 ....$17.95

Songs Of Love
58 romantic ballads, including: All The Things You Are • Can You Feel The Love Tonight • A Fine Romance • Friends & Lovers • Have I Told You Lately • I Swear • Misty • The Power Of Love • Saving All My Love For You • Truly • When I Fall In Love • A Whole New World • and more.
00311704 ....$15.95

Songs Of Romance
35 romantic favorites, including: All I Ask Of You • And I Love Her • Can't Smile Without You • Could I Have This Dance • Don't Know Much • Endless Love • Feelings • Forever And Ever Amen • Hopelessly Devoted To You • How Am I Supposed To Live Without You • How Deep Is Your Love • Imagine • I'll Be Loving You (Forever) • Just The Way You Are • Longer • Sometimes When We Touch • Somewhere Out There • You Decorated My Life • more.
00490361 ....$12.95

Today's Love Songs
31 of today's sentimental favorites, including: All I Ask Of You • Because I Love You • Don't Know Much • Endless Love • Every Heartbeat • Lost In Your Eyes • Vision Of Love • and more. 160 pages.
00311550 ....$14.95

The Wedding And Love Collection
A collection of 33 beautiful contemporary hits and standards, including: Ave Maria • Don't Know Much • Endless Love • Longer • The Lord's Prayer • Lost In Your Eyes • Sunrise, Sunset • The Vows Go Unbroken • Walk Forever By My Side • much more.
00490377 ....$12.95

Wedding Songs Of Love & Friendship
28 love songs appropriate for use in Christian services. Features: Always • Doubly Good To You • Let Us Climb The Hill Together • Longer • The Lord's Prayer • Sunrise, Sunset • Wedding Prayer • What A Difference You've Made In My Life.
00361489 ....$10.95